From the Library
with every good
wish.
Wednesday, April 8th – 19

Best wishes ever!
Mary Sterling

KARMA

A STORY OF

BUDDHIST ETHICS

BY

PAUL CARUS

ILLUSTRATED BY KWASON SUZUKI

COMMIT NO EVIL; BUT DO GOOD
AND LET THY HEART BE PURE.
THAT IS THE GIST OF BUDDHAHOOD,
THE LORE THAT WILL ENDURE.
—THE DHAMMAPADA, 183

SIXTH EDITION

CHICAGO :: LONDON
OPEN COURT PUBLISHING COMPANY
1917

COPYRIGHT, 1894
OPEN COURT PUBLISHING COMPANY
CHICAGO

PRINTED IN THE UNITED STATES OF AMERICA

PUBLISHERS' ADVERTISEMENT.

> "All are needed by each one;
> Nothing is fair or good alone."
> —*Emerson*.

SOON after the first appearance of *Karma* in the columns of *The Open Court*, several applications to translate the story were received, and the requests granted. Some of these translations have appeared, others may still be expected. A few translations were made without the author's knowledge. A German edition was published by the Open Court Publishing Co. Altogether one Japanese, one Urdu, three German, and two French renderings are at present in the author's possession. It is possible that the story also exists in Icelandic,[1] Tamil, Singhalese, and Siamese versions. A Hungarian edition is in preparation.

A Russian translation was made by Count Leo Tolstoy, who recommends the story to his countrymen and sums up his opinion as follows:

"This tale has greatly pleased me both by its artlessness and its profundity. The truth, much slurred in these days, that evil

---

[1] An Icelandic translation has been made by the Rev. Matthias Jochumson of Akureyri, Iceland, and must have appeared in the Icelandic periodical of which he is editor, but we do not know whether it has appeared in book-form.

can be avoided and good achieved by personal effort only and that there exists no other means of attaining this end, has here been shown forth with striking clearness. The explanation is felicitous in that it proves that individual happiness is never genuine save when it is bound up with the happiness of all our fellows. From the very moment when the brigand on escaping from Hell thought only of his own happiness, his happiness ceased and he fell back again into his former doom.

"This Buddhistic tale seems to shed light on a new side of the two fundamental truths revealed by Christianity: that life exists only in the renunciation of one's personality—'he that loseth his life shall find it' (Matt. x. 39), and, that the good of men is only in their union with God, and through God with one another —'As thou art in me and I in thee, that they also may be one in us' (John xvii. 21).

"I have read this tale to children and they liked it. And amongst grown-up people its reading always gave rise to conversation about the gravest problems of life. And, to my mind, this is the very best recommendation."

From the Russian the story *Karma* was translated, together with several other sketches, by E. Halpérine-Kaminsky, under the title *Imitations*, and the work was published under Tolstoy's name at Paris by the *Société d'éditions littéraires et artistiques*.[1]

Either from Tolstoy's Russian version or from the French translation, an abbreviated German translation was made by an author who signs himself "*y*," and this appeared in the *Berliner Evangelisches Sonntagsblatt*, May 2, 1897 (No. 18, pp. 140–141). Here, too, the story goes under Tolstoy's name.

[1] Librairie Paul Ollendorff, 50, Chaussée d'Antin, 1900.

While the evangelical Sunday paper reproduces *Karma* as a story that inculcates Christian principles, the late Professor Ludwig Büchner, famous as the author of the leading materialistic work, *Force and Matter* (*Kraft und Stoff*), translated *Karma* from the English under the impression that he had before him some mysterious ancient Buddhist document, for he calls it "an Indian tale from the English of the *P. C.*" Apparently he mistook the signature *P. C.*, over which the story first appeared, for an abbreviated title of some forgotten *P*âli *C*odex or *P*undit *C*ollection, and at any rate a *P*agan *C*uriosity. It appeared in *Ethische Kultur*, the organ of the German Ethical Societies, Berlin, June 1 and 8, 1895 (Vol. III., Nos. 22 and 23).

Having appeared under Tolstoy's name in French and in German, the story continued in its further migrations to sail under the famous Russian author's name. An enterprising American periodical entitled *The International Magazine* published an English translation in Chicago, and it is curious that the office of this journal was in the very same block with that of The Open Court Publishing Company. So the story had completed its rounds through Russia, Germany, and France, and had returned to its home in the far West.

Since the story had gained currency under Tolstoy's name, the author (having previously had correspondence with him) wrote to Posnia, and Tolstoy replied expressing his regret at the misunderstanding saying of *Karma:*

"It was only through your letter that I learned it had been circulated under my name, and I deeply regret, not only that such a falsehood was allowed to pass unchallenged, but also the fact that it really was a falsehood, for I should be very happy were I the author of this tale. It is one of the best products of national wisdom and ought to be bequeathed to all mankind, like the Odyssey, the History of Joseph, and Shakyamuni."

Karma appeared first in book form in Japan, where The Open Court Publishing Company brought out at Hasegawa's three successive editions on crêpe paper, illustrated in colors by Kwason Suzuki. In the present edition the Japanese illustrations, which were retouched by Eduard Biedermann, are reproduced in black and white, and we hope that the artistic garb will do much to make the little tale attractive.

THE OPEN COURT PUBLISHING CO.

DÊVALA'S RICE-CART.

LONG, long ago in the days of early Buddhism, India was in a most prosperous condition. The Aryan inhabitants of the country were highly civilised, and the great cities were centres of industry, commerce, and learning.

It was in those olden times that Pandu, a wealthy jeweller of the Brahman caste, travelled in a carriage to Bârânasî, which is now called Benares. He was bent on some lucrative banking business, and a slave who attended to the horses accompanied him.

The jeweller was apparently in a hurry to reach his destination, and as the day was exceedingly pleasant, since a heavy thunderstorm had cooled the atmosphere, the horses sped along rapidly.

While proceeding on their journey the travellers overtook a samana, as the Buddhist monks were called, and the jeweller observing the venerable appearance of the holy man, thought to himself: "This samana looks noble and saintly. Companionship with good men brings luck; should he also be going to Bârânasî, I will invite him to ride with me in my carriage."

Having saluted the samana the jeweller explained whither he was driving and at what inn he intended to stay in Bârânasî. Learning that the samana, whose name was Nârada, also was travelling to Bârânasî, he asked him to accept a seat in his carriage. "I am obliged to you for your kindness," said the samana to the Brahman, "for I am quite worn out by the long journey. As I have no possessions in this world, I cannot repay you in money; but it may happen that I can reward you with some spiritual treasure out of the wealth of the information I have received while following Shâkyamuni, the Blessed One, the Great Buddha, the Teacher of gods and men."

They travelled together in the carriage and Pandu listened with pleasure to the instructive discourse of Nârada. After about an hour's journey, they arrived at a place where the road had been rendered almost impassable

by a washout caused by the recent rain, and a farmer's cart heavily laden with rice prevented further progress. The loss of a linchpin had caused one of the wheels to come off, and Dêvala, the owner of the cart, was busily engaged in repairing the damage. He, too, was on his way to Bârânasî to sell his rice, and was anxious to reach the city before the dawn of the next morning. If he was delayed a day or two longer, the rice merchants might have left town or bought all the stock they needed.

When the jeweller saw that he could not proceed on his way unless the farmer's cart was removed, he began to grow angry and ordered Mahâduta, his slave, to push the cart aside, so that his carriage could pass by. The farmer remonstrated because, being so near the slope of the road, it would jeopardise his cargo; but the Brahman would not listen to the farmer and bade his servant overturn the rice-cart and push it aside. Mahâduta, an unusually strong man, who seemed to take delight in the injury of others, obeyed before the samana could interfere. The rice was thrown on the wayside, and the farmer's plight was worse than before.

The poor farmer began to scold, but when

the big, burly Mahâduta raised his fist threateningly, he ceased his remonstrances and only growled his curses in a low undertone.

When Pandu was about to continue his journey the samana jumped out of the carriage and said: "'Excuse me, sir, for leaving you here. I am under obligations for your kindness in giving me an hour's ride in your carriage. I was tired when you picked me up on the road, but now, thanks to your courtesy, I am rested, and recognising in this farmer an incarnation of one of your ancestors, I cannot repay your kindness better than by assisting him in his troubles."

The Brahman jeweller looked at the samana in amazement: "That farmer, you say, is an incarnation of one of my ancestors? That is impossible!"

"I know," replied the samana, "that you are not aware of the numerous important relations which tie your fate to that of the farmer; but sometimes the smartest men are spiritually blind. So I regret that you harm your own interests, and I shall try to protect you against the wounds which you are about to inflict upon yourself."

The wealthy merchant was not accustomed to being reprimanded, and feeling that the words of the samana, although uttered with great kindness, contained a stinging reproach, bade his servant drive on without further delay.

THE JEWELLER'S PURSE.

THE samana saluted Dêvala, the farmer, and began to help him repair his cart and load up the rice, part of which had been thrown out. The work proceeded quickly and Dêvala thought: "This samana must be a holy man; invisible devas[1] seem to assist him. I will ask him how I deserved ill treatment at the hands of the proud Brahman." And he said: "Venerable sir, can you tell me why I suffer an injustice from a man to whom I have never done any harm?"

And the samana said: "My dear friend, you do not suffer an injustice, but only receive in your present state of existence the same treatment which you visited upon the jeweller in a former life. You reap what you have sown, and your fate is the product of your deeds. Your very existence, such as it is now, is but the Karma of your past lives."

"What is my Karma?" asked the farmer.

"A man's Karma," replied the samana, "consists of all the deeds both good and evil

that he has done in his present and in any prior existence. Your life is a system of many activities which have originated in the natural process of evolution, and have been transferred from generation to generation. The entire being of every one of us is an accumulation of inherited functions which are modified by new experiences and deeds. Thus we are what we have done. Our 'Karma' constitutes our nature. We are our own creators."

"That may be as you say," rejoined Dêvala, "but what have I to do with that overbearing Brahman?"

The samana replied: "You are in character quite similar to the Brahman, and the Karma that has shaped your destiny differs but little from his. If I am not mistaken in reading your thoughts, I should say that you would, even to-day, have done the same unto the jeweller if he had been in your place, and if you had such a strong slave at your command as he has, able to deal with you at his pleasure."

The farmer confessed, that if he had had the power, he would have felt little compunction in treating another man, who had happened to impede his way, as he had been treated by the Brahman, but thinking of the retribution attendant upon unkind deeds, he resolved to be in the future more considerate with his fellow-beings.

The rice was loaded and together they pursued their journey to Bârânasî, when sud-

denly the horse jumped aside. "A snake, a snake!" shouted the farmer; but the samana looked closely at the object at which the horse shuddered, jumped out of the cart, and saw that it was a purse full of gold, and the idea struck him: "This money can belong to no one but the wealthy jeweller."

Nârada took the purse and found that it contained a goodly sum of gold pieces. Then he said to the farmer: "Now is the time for you to teach the proud jeweller a lesson, and it will redound to your well-being both in this and in future lives. No revenge is sweeter than the requital of hatred with deeds of good will.[2] I will give you this purse, and when you come to Bârânasî drive up to the inn which I shall point out to you; ask for Pandu, the Brahman, and deliver to him his gold. He will excuse himself for the rudeness with which he treated you, but tell him that you have forgiven him and wish him success in all his undertakings. For, let me tell you, the more successful he is, the better you will prosper; your fate depends in many respects upon his fate. Should the jeweller demand any explanation, send him to the vihâra[3] where he will find me ready to assist him with advice in case he may feel the need of it."

BUSINESS IN BENARES.

To corner the market of the necessities of life is not a modern invention. The Old Testament contains the story of Joseph, the poor Hebrew youth who became minister of state, and succeeded with unscrupulous but clever business tricks in cornering the wheat market, so as to force the starved people to sell all their property, their privileges, and even their lives, to Pharaoh. And we read in the Jâtaka Tales[1] that one of the royal treasurers of Kâsî, which is the old name of Bârânasî, made his first great success in life by cornering the grass market of the metropolis on the day of the arrival of a horse dealer with five hundred horses.

When Pandu the jeweller arrived at Bârânasî it so happened that a bold speculator had brought about a corner in rice, and Mallika, a rich banker and a business friend of Pandu, was in great distress. On meeting the jeweller he said: "I am a ruined man and can do no business with you unless I can buy a cart of the best rice for the king's table. I have a rival banker in Bârânasî who, learning that I had made a contract with the royal treasurer to deliver the rice to-morrow morning, and being desirous to bring about my destruction, has bought up all the rice in Bârânasî. The royal treasurer must have received a bribe, for he will not release me from my contract, and to-morrow I shall be a ruined man unless Krishna[5] will send an angel from heaven to help me."

While Mallika was still lamenting the poverty to which his rival would reduce him, Pandu missed his purse. Searching his carriage without being able to find it, he suspected his slave Mahâduta; and calling the police, accused him of theft, and had him bound and cruelly tortured to extort a confession.

The slave in his agonies cried: "I am innocent, let me go, for I cannot stand this pain; I am quite innocent, at least of this crime, and suffer now for other sins. Oh, that I could beg the farmer's pardon whom, for the sake of my master, I wronged without any cause! This torture, I believe, is a punishment for my rudeness."

While the officer was still applying the lash to the back of the slave, the farmer arrived at the inn and, to the great astonishment of all concerned, delivered the purse. The slave was at once released from the hands of his torturer. But being dissatisfied with his master, he secretly left and joined a band of robbers in the mountains, who made him their chief on account of his great strength and courage.

When Mallika heard that the farmer had the best rice to sell, fit for delivery to the royal table, he at once bought the whole cart-load for treble the price that the farmer had ever received. Pandu, however, glad at heart to have his money restored, rewarded the honest finder, and hastened at once to the vihâra to receive further explanation from Nârada, the samana.

Nârada said: "I might give you an explanation, but knowing that you are unable to understand a spiritual truth, I prefer to remain silent. Yet I shall give you some advice: Treat every man whom you meet as your own self; serve him as you would demand to be served yourself; for our Karma travels; it walks apace though, and the journey is often long. But be it good or evil, finally it will come home to us. Therefore it is said:

> 'Slowly but surely deeds
> Home to the doer creep.
> Of kindness sow thy seeds,
> And bliss as harvest reap.'"

"Give me, O samana, the explanation," said the jeweller, "and I shall thereby be better able to follow your advice."

The samana said: "Listen then, I will give you the key to the mystery. If you do not understand it, have faith in what I say. Self is an illusion, and he whose mind is bent upon following self, follows a will-o'-the-wisp which leads him into the quagmire of sin. The illusion of self is like dust in your eye that blinds your sight and prevents you from recognising the close relations that obtain between yourself and your fellows, which are even closer than the relations that obtain among the various organs of your body. You must learn to trace the identity of your self in the souls of other beings. Ignorance is the source of sin. There are few who know the truth. Let this motto be your talisman:

> 'Who injureth others
> Himself hurteth sore;
> Who others assisteth
> Himself helpeth more.
> Let th' illusion of self
> From your mind disappear,
> And you'll find the way sure;
> The path will be clear.'

"To him whose vision is dimmed by the dust of the world, the spiritual life appears to be cut up into innumerable selves. Thus he will be puzzled in many ways concerning the nature of rebirth, and will be incapable of understanding the import of an all-comprehensive loving-kindness toward all living beings."

The jeweller replied: "Your words, O venerable sir, have a deep significance and I shall bear them in mind. I extended a small kindness which caused me no expense whatever, to a poor samana on my way to Bârânasî, and lo! how propitious has been the result! I am deeply in your debt, for without you I should not only have lost my purse, but would have been prevented from doing business in

Bârânasî which greatly increases my wealth, while if it had been left undone it might have reduced me to a state of wretched poverty. In addition, your thoughtfulness and the arrival of the farmer's rice-cart preserved the prosperity of my friend Mallika, the banker. If all men saw the truth of your maxims, how much better the world would be! Evils would be lessened, and public welfare enhanced."

The samana replied: "Among all the religions there is none like that of the Buddha. It is glorious in the beginning, glorious in the middle, and glorious in the end. It is glorious in the letter and glorious in the spirit.[6] It is the religion of loving-kindness that rids man of the narrowness of egotism and elevates him above his petty self to the bliss of enlightenment which manifests itself in righteousness."

Pandu nodded assent and said: "As I am anxious to let the truth of the Buddha be understood, I shall found a vihâra at my native place, Kaushambî, and invite you to visit me, so that I may dedicate the place to the brotherhood of Buddha's disciples."

AMONG THE ROBBERS.

YEARS passed on and Pandu's vihâra at Kaushambî became a place in which wise samanas used to stay and it was renowned as a centre of enlightenment for the people of the town.

At that time the king of a neighboring country had heard of the beauty of Pandu's jewelry, and he sent his treasurer to order a royal diadem to be wrought in pure gold and set with the most precious stones of India. Pandu gladly accepted the order and executed a crown of the most exquisite design. When he had finished the work, he started for the residence of the king, and as he expected to transact other profitable business, took with him a great store of gold pieces.

The caravan carrying his goods was protected by a strong escort of armed men, but when they reached the mountains they were attacked by a band of robbers led by Mahâduta, who beat them and took away all the jewelry and the gold, and Pandu escaped with

great difficulty. This calamity was a blow to Pandu's prosperity, and as he had suffered some other severe losses his wealth was greatly reduced.

Pandu was much distressed, but he bore his misfortunes without complaint, thinking to himself: "I have deserved these losses for the sins committed during my past existence.

In my younger years I was very hard on other people; because I now reap the harvest of my evil deeds I have no reason for complaint."

As he had grown in kindness toward all beings, his misfortunes only served to purify his heart; and his chief regret, when thinking of his reduced means, was that he had be-

come unable to do good and to help his friends in the vihâra to spread the truths of religion.

Again years passed on and it happened that

Panthaka, a young samana and disciple of Nârada, was travelling through the mountains of Kaushambî, and he fell among the robbers in the mountains. As he had nothing in his possession, the robber-chief beat him severely and let him go.

On the next morning Panthaka, while pursuing his way through the woods, heard a noise as of men quarelling and fighting, and going to the place he saw a number of robbers, all of them in a great rage, and in their midst stood Mahâduta, their chief; and Mahâduta was desperately defending himself against them, like a lion surrounded by hounds, and he slew several of his aggressors with formidable blows, but there were too many for him; at last he succumbed and fell to the ground as if dead, covered with wounds.

As soon as the robbers had left the place, the young samana approached to see whether he could be of any assistance to the wounded men. He found that all the robbers were dead, and there was but little life left in the chief.

At once Panthaka went down to the little

brooklet which was murmuring near by, fetched fresh water in his bowl and brought it to the dying man. Mahâduta opened his eyes and gnashing his teeth, said: "Where are those ungrateful dogs whom I have led to victory and success? Without me as their chief they will soon perish like jackals hunted down by skilful hunters."

"Do not think of your comrades, the companions of your sinful life," said Panthaka, "but think of your own fate, and accept in the last moment the chance of salvation that is offered you. Here is water to drink, and let me dress your wounds; perhaps I may save your life."

"Alas! alas!" replied Mahâduta, "are you not the man whom I beat but yesterday? And now you come to my assistance, to assuage my pain! You bring me fresh water to quench my thirst, and try to save my life! It is useless, honorable sir, I am a doomed man. The churls have wounded me unto death,— the ungrateful cowards! They have dealt me the blow which I taught them."

"You reap what you have sown," continued

the samana; "had you taught your comrades acts of kindness, you would have received from them acts of kindness; but having taught them the lesson of slaughter, it is but your own deed that you are slain by their hands."

"True, very true," said the robber chief, "my fate is well deserved; but how sad is my lot, that I must reap the full harvest of all my evil deeds in future existences! Advise me, O holy sir, what I can do to lighten the sins of my life which oppress me like a great rock placed upon my breast, taking away the breath from my lungs."

Said Panthaka: "Root out your sinful desires; destroy all evil passions, and fill your heart with kindness toward all your fellow-beings."

THE SPIDER-WEB.

WHILE the charitable samana washed the wounds, the robber chief said: "I have done much evil and no good. How can I extricate myself from the net of sorrow which I have woven out of the evil desires of my own heart? My Karma will lead me to Hell and I shall never be able to walk in the path of salvation."

Said the samana: "Indeed your Karma will in its future incarnations reap the seeds of evil that you have sown. There is no escape from the consequences of our actions. But there is no cause for despair. The man who is converted and has rooted out the illusion of self, with all its lusts and sinful desires, will be a source of blessing to himself and others.

"As an illustration, I will tell you the story of the great robber Kandata, who died with-

26   KARMA.

out repentance and was reborn as a demon in

Hell, where he suffered for his evil deeds the most terrible agonies and pains. He had been in Hell several kalpas[7] and was unable to rise out of his wretched condition, when Buddha appeared upon earth and attained to the blessed state of enlightenment. At that memorable moment a ray of light fell down into Hell quickening all the demons with life and hope, and the robber Kandata cried aloud: 'O blessed Buddha, have mercy upon me! I suffer greatly, and although I have done evil, I am anxious to walk in the noble path of righteousness. But I cannot extricate myself from the net of sorrow. Help me, O Lord; have mercy on me!'

"Now, it is the law of Karma that evil deeds lead to destruction, for absolute evil is so bad that it cannot exist. Absolute evil involves impossibility of existence. But good deeds lead to life. Thus there is a final end to every deed that is done, but there is no end to the development of good deeds. The least act of goodness bears fruit containing new seeds of goodness, and they continue to grow, they nourish the poor suffering creatures in their repeated wanderings in the eternal round of Samsâra[3] until they reach the final deliverance from all evil in Nirvâna.

"When Buddha, the Lord, heard the prayer of the demon suffering in Hell, he said: 'Kandata, did you ever perform an act of kindness? It will now return to you and help you to rise again. But you cannot be rescued unless the intense sufferings which you endure as consequences of your evil deeds have dispelled all conceit of selfhood and have purified your soul of vanity, lust, and envy.'

"Kandata remained silent, for he had been a cruel man, but the Tathâgata in his omniscience saw all the deeds done by the poor wretch, and he perceived that once in his life when walking through the woods he had seen a spider crawling on the ground, and he thought to himself, 'I will not step upon the spider, for he is a harmless creature and hurts nobody.'

"Buddha looked with compassion upon the tortures of Kandata, and sent down a spider on a cobweb and the spider said: 'Take hold of the web and climb up.'

"Having attached the web at the bottom of

Hell, the spider withdrew. Kandata eagerly

seized the thin thread and made great efforts
to climb up. And he succeeded. The web

was so strong that it held, and he ascended higher and higher.

"Suddenly he felt the thread trembling and shaking, for behind him some of his fellow-sufferers were beginning to climb up. Kandata became frightened. He saw the thinness of the web, and observed that it was elastic, for under the increased weight it stretched out; yet it still seemed strong enough to carry him. Kandata had heretofore only looked up; he now looked down, and saw following close upon his heels, also climbing up on the cobweb, a numberless mob of the denizens of Hell. 'How can this thin thread bear the weight of all?' he thought to himself, and seized with fear he shouted loudly: 'Let go the cobweb. It is mine!'

"At once the cobweb broke, and Kandata fell back into Hell.

"'The illusion of self was still upon Kandata. He did not know the miraculous power of a sincere longing to rise upwards and enter the noble path of righteousness. It is thin like a cobweb, but it will carry millions of people, and the more there are that climb it, the easier will be the efforts of every one of them. But as soon as the idea arises in a man's heart: 'This is mine; let the bliss of righteousness be mine alone, and let no one else partake of it,' the thread breaks and he will fall back into his old condition of selfhood. For selfhood is damnation, and truth is bliss. What is Hell? It is nothing but egotism, and Nirvâna is a life of righteousness."

"Let me take hold of the spider-web," said the dying robber chief, when the samana had finished his story, "and I will pull myself up out of the depths of Hell."

THE CONVERSION OF THE ROBBER CHIEF.

MAHÂDUTA lay quiet for a while to collect his thoughts, and then he addressed the samana not without effort:

"Listen, honorable sir, I will make a confession: I was the servant of Pandu, the jeweller of Kaushambî, but when he unjustly had me tortured I ran away and became a chief of robbers. Some time ago when I heard from my spies that Pandu was passing through the mountains, I succeeded in robbing him of a great part of his wealth. Will you now go to him and tell him that I have forgiven from the bottom of my heart the injury which he unjustly inflicted upon me, and ask him, too, to pardon me for having robbed him. While I stayed with him his heart was as hard as flint, and I learned to imitate the selfishness of his character. I have heard that he has become benevolent and is now pointed out as an example of goodness and justice. He has laid up treasures of which no robber can ever de-

prive him,⁹ while I fear that my Karma will continue to linger in the course of evil deeds; but I do not wish to remain in his debt so long as it is still in my power to pay him. My heart has undergone a complete change. My evil passions are subdued, and the few moments of life left me shall be spent in the endeavor to continue after death in the good Karma of righteous aspirations. Therefore, inform Pandu that I have kept the gold crown which he wrought for the king, and all his treasures, and have hidden them in a cave near by. There were only two of the robbers under my command who knew of it, and both are now dead. Let Pandu take a number of armed men and come to the place and take back the property of which I have deprived him. One act of justice will atone for some of my sins; it will help to cleanse my soul of its impurities and give me a start in the right direction on my search for salvation."

Then Mahâduta described the location of the cave and fell back exhausted.

For a while he lay with closed eyes as though sleeping. The pain of his wounds had ceased, and he began to breathe quietly; but his life was slowly ebbing away, and now he seemed to awake as from a pleasant dream.

CONVERSION OF THE ROBBER CHIEF. 35

"Venerable sir," said he, "what a blessing for me that the Buddha came upon earth and taught you and caused our paths to meet and made you comfort me. While I lay dozing I

beheld as in a vision the scene of the Tathâgata's final entering into Nirvâna. In former years I saw a picture of it which made a deep impression on my mind, and the recollection of it is a solace to me in my dying hour."

"Indeed, it is a blessing," replied the samana, "that the Buddha appeared upon earth; he dispelled the darkness begotten by ill will and error, and attained supreme enlightenment. He lived among us as one of us, being subject to the ills of life, pain, disease, and death, not unlike any mortal. Yet he extinguished in himself all selfishness, all lust, all greed for wealth and love of pleasure, all ambition for fame or power, all hankering after things of the world and clinging to anything transitory and illusive. He was bent only on the one aim, to reach the immortal and to actualise in his being that which cannot die. Through the good Karma of former existences and his own life he reached at last the blessed state of Nirvâna, and when the end came he passed away in that final passing away which leaves nothing behind but extinguishes all that is transitory and mortal. Oh, that all men could give up clinging and thereby rid themselves of passion, envy, and hatred!"

Mahâduta imbibed the words of the samana with the eagerness of a thirsty man who is refreshed by a drink of water that is pure and cool and sweet. He wanted to speak, but he could scarcely rally strength enough to open his mouth and move his lips. He beckoned assent and showed his anxiety to embrace the doctrine of the Tathâgata.

Panthaka wetted the dying man's lips and soothed his pain, and when the robber chief, unable to speak, silently folded his hands, he spoke for him and gave utterance to such vows as the latter was ready to make. The samana's words were like music to the ears of Mahâduta. Filled with the joy that originates with good resolutions and entranced by the prospect of an advance in the search for a higher and better life, his eyes began to stare and all pain ceased.

So the robber chief died converted in the arms of the samana.

THE CONVERTED ROBBER'S TOMB.

AS soon as Panthaka, the young samana, had reached Kaushambî, he went to the vihâra and inquired for Pandu the jeweller. Being directed to his residence he gave him a full account of his recent adventure in the forest. And Pandu set out with an escort of armed men and secured the treasures which the robber chief had concealed in the cave. Near by they found the remains of the robber chief and his slain comrades, and they gathered the bodies in a heap and burned them with all honors.

The ashes were collected in an urn and buried in a tumulus on which a stone was placed with an inscription written by Panthaka, which contained a brief report of Mahâduta's conversion.

Before Pandu's party returned home, Panthaka held a memorial service at the tumulus

THE CONVERTED ROBBER'S TOMB. 39

in which he explained the significance of Karma, discoursing on the words of Buddha:

"By ourselves is evil done,
By ourselves we pain endure.
By ourselves we cease from wrong,
By ourselves become we pure.

> No one saves us, but ourselves,
> No one can and no one may:
> We ourselves must walk the path,
> Buddhas merely teach the way."[10]

"Our Karma," the samana said, "is not the work of Ishvara, or Brahma, or Indra, or of any one of the gods. Our Karma is the product of our own actions. My action is the womb that bears me; it is the inheritance which devolves upon me; it is the curse of my misdeeds and the blessing of my righteousness. My action is the resource by which alone I can work out my salvation."[11]

Then the samana paused and added:

"While every one is the maker of his own Karma, and we reap what we have sown, we are at the same time co-responsible for the evils of evil doers. Such is the interrelation of Karma that the errors of one person are mostly mere echoes of the errors of others. Neither the curse of our failings nor the bliss of our goodness is purely our own. Therefore when we judge the bad, the vicious, the criminal, let us not withhold from them our sympathy, for we are partners of their guilt."

Among the people of the surrounding villages the tumulus became known as "The Converted Robber's Tomb," and in later years a little shrine was built on the spot where wanderers used to rest and invoke the Buddha for the conversion of robbers and thieves.

THE BEQUEST OF A GOOD KARMA.

PANDU carried all his treasures back to Kaushambî, and using with discretion the wealth thus unexpectedly regained, he became richer and more powerful than he had ever been before, and when he was dying at an advanced age he had all his sons, and daughters, and grandchildren gathered round him and said unto them:

"My dear children, do not blame others for your lack of success. Seek the cause of your ills in yourselves. Unless you are blinded by vanity you will discover your fault, and having discovered it you will see the way out of it. The remedy for your ills, too, lies in yourselves. Never let your mental eyes be covered by the dust of selfishness, and remember the words which have proved a talisman in my life:

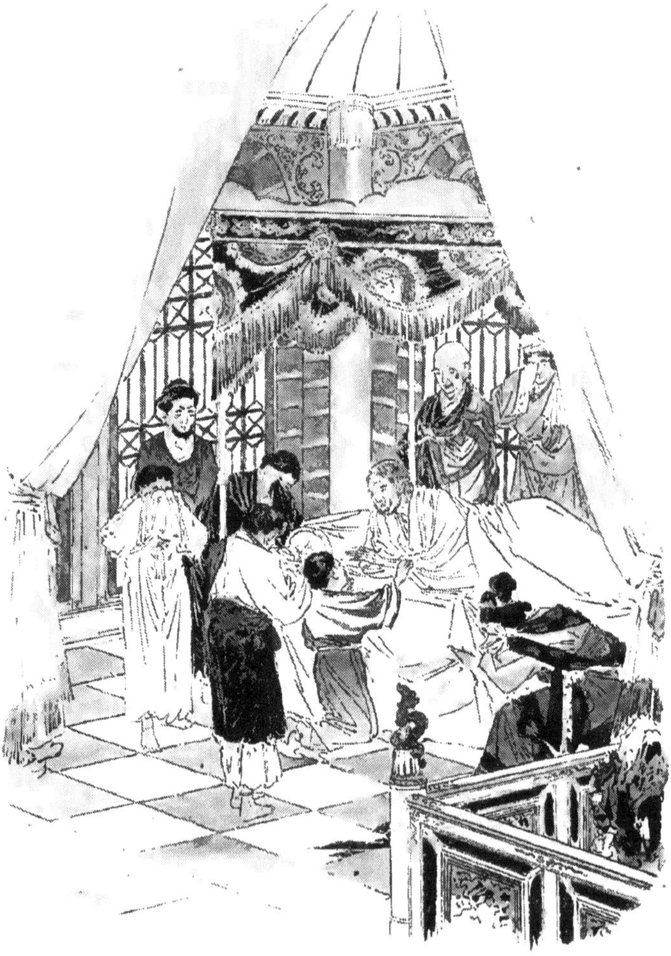

'Who injureth others,
　Himself hurteth sore.
　Who others assisteth,
　Himself helpeth more.
　Let th' illusion of self
　From your mind disappear:
　And you'll find the way sure;
　The path will be clear.'

"If you heed my words and obey these injunctions you will, when you come to die, continue to live in the Good Karma that you have stored up, and your souls will be immortalised according to your deeds."

NOTES.

1, Page 7.

Devas are spiritual beings, gods, or angels.

2, Page 11.

This sentiment, though thoroughly Buddhistic, is found also in other religions and seems to grow naturally when a certain moral maturity is reached.

Every one knows the passage in the Gospel according to Matthew: "But I say unto you, Love your enemies."

Lao Tze (V., 44) the sage of China said: 報怨以德 *pao yuen i teh*, i. e., "Requite hatred with virtue."

And Socrates expressed himself no less plainly in Plato's *Crito*, 49:

Οὔτε ἀνταδικεῖν δεῖ, οὔτε κακῶς ποιεῖν οὐδένα ἀνθρώπων, οὐδ' ἂν ὁτιοῦν πάσχῃ ὑπ' αὐτῶν.

One must neither return evil, nor do any ill to any one among men, not even if one has to suffer from them.

See *The Open Court* for January, 1901, p. 9, for further quotations from the Greek.

3, Page 11.

Buddhist monastery.

4, Page 12.

Buddhist Birth Stories. Translated by T. W. Rhys Davids, p. 169.

5, Page 13.

Krishna, a Brahman god, an incarnation of Vishnu, the second person of the Brahman trinity. Mallika's language implies that he is not a Buddhist.

6, Page 18.

This passage occurs in the Mahâvagga, I., 2.

7, Page 27.

Kalpa is a long period of time, an æon.

8, Page 28.

Samsâra is the restlessness of the world and of worldly life, Nirvâna is the peace of mind of him who has overcome the illusion of self.

9, Page 33.

This expression reminding one of Matth. vi. 20, is taken from the Nidhikanda Sutta (Treasure Chapter).

10, Page 40.

Quoted from the *Dhammapada*

11, Page 40.

Quoted from the Anguttara Nikâya, Pañcaka Nipâta, see Oldenberg, *Buddha*, p. 249.

Works by Dr. Paul Carus

The Age of Christ.
A brief review of the conditions under which Christianity originated. Paper, 15c.

Amitabha, A Story of Buddnist Theology.
Boards, 50c.

Angelus Silesius.
A selection from the rhymes of a German mystic. Translated in the original meter. Cloth, $1.00;

The Bride of Christ.
A study in Christian legend lore. Illustrated. Cloth, 75c.

The Buddha.
A drama in three acts and four interludes. Paper, 50c.

Buddhism and Its Christian Critics.
Cloth, $1.25; paper, 60c.

Buddhist Hymns.
Translated from the Dhammapada and other sources adapted to modern music. Cloth, 50c.

Canon of Reason and Virtue (Lao-Tze's Tao Teh King.)
Chinese-English. New and revised edition. Cloth, $1.00.

The Chief's Daughter.
A legend of Niagara. Illustrated. Cloth, $1.00.

Chinese Life and Customs.
With illustrations by Chinese artists. Boards, 75c.

Chinese Thought.
An exposition of the main characteristic features of the Chinese world-conception. Being a continuation of the author's essay "Chinese Philosophy." Illustrated. Boards, $1.00.

The Crown of Thorns.
A story of the time of Christ. Illustrated. Cloth, 75c.

The Dawn of a New Religious Era.
And other essays. Cloth, $1.00.

The Pleroma.
An essay on the origin of Christianity. Cloth, $1.00; paper, 50c.

Primer of Philosophy.
Cloth, $1.00; paper, 30c.

Edward's Dream.
Translated and edited from the German of Wilhelm Busch. Cloth, $1.00.

Eros and Psyche.
A fairy-tale of ancient Greece, re-told after Apuleins. Illustrated. Cloth, $1.50.

The Ethical Problem.
Three lectures on ethics as a science. Cloth, $1.25; paper, 60c.

The Foundations of Mathematics.
A contribution to the philosophy of geometry. Cloth, 75c.

Frederich Schiller.
A sketch of his life and an appreciation of his poetry. Profusely illustrated. Boards, 75c.

Fundamental Problems.
The method of philosophy as a systematic arrangement of knowledge. Cltoh, $1.50; paper, 60c.

God.
An inquiry into the nature of Man's Highest Ideal and a solution of the problem from the standpoint of science. Boards, $1.00; paper, 50c.

Godward.
A record of religious progress. (Poems). Cloth, 50c.

Goethe.
With special consideration of his philosophy. Profusely illustrated. Cloth, $3.00.

Goethe and Schiller's Xenions.
New and revised edition, with additional notes on classical prosody in the Introduction. Cloth, $1.00.

The Gospel of Buddha.
According to old records. Cloth, $1.00; paper, 40c.

Gospel of Buddha.
Pocket edition. Photographic reproduction of the de Luxe edition which is out of print. Price, Cloth $1.00. Leather at $1.50.

The History of the Devil and the Idea of Evil.
From the earliest times to the present day. Illustrated. Cloth, $6.00.

Kant and Spencer.
A study of the fallacies of agnosticism. Cloth, 50c; paper, 25c.

Kant's Prolegomena to any Future Metaphysics.
Cloth, 75c; paper, 60c.

K'ung Fu Tze.
A dramatic poem portraying the life and teachings of Confucius. Boards, 50c.

Lao-Tze's Tao Teh King.
Chinese English. With introduction, literal translation and notes. Cloth, $3.00.

Works by Dr. Paul Carus

The Mechanistic Principle and the Non-Mechanical.
An inquiry into fundamentals with extracts from representatives of either side. Cloth, $1.00.

The Nature of the State.
Cloth, 50c; paper, 20c.

The New Morn.
A dramatic poem satirizing English diplomacy and the Triple Entente. Paper, 50c.

Nietzsche.
And other exponents of individualism. Illustrated. Cloth, $1.25.

Nirvana, a Story of Buddhist Psychology.
Illustrated by Kwason Suzuki. Cloth, 60c.

Oracle of Yahveh.
Urim and Thummim, the Ephod, the Breastplate of Judgment. Illustrated. Paper, 30c.

Our Children.
Hints from practical experience for parents and teachers. Cloth, $1.00.

Personality.
With special reference to super-personalities and the interpersonal character of ideas. Cloth, 75c.

The Philosopher's Martyrdom.
A satire. Illustrated. Boards, $1.00; parchment wrapper, 50c.

Philosophy of Science.
An Epitome of the writings of Dr. Paul Carus. Boards, 50c; paper, 25c.

The Principle of Relativity.
In the light of the philosophy of science. Cloth, $1.00.

Psychology of the Nervous System.
An extract from the author's larger work "The Soul of Man." Paper, 30c.

Yin Chih Wen.
The Tract of the Quiet Way. With extracts from the Chinese Commentary. Boards, 25c.

The Rise of Man.
A sketch of the origin of the human race. Illustrated. Boards, 75c.

Sacred Tunes for the Consecration of Life.
Hymns of the Religion of Science. Cloth, 50c.

The Soul of Man.
An investigation of the facts of physiological and experimental psychology. Illustrated. Cloth, $1.50; papr, 85c.

The Story of Samson.
And its place in the religious development of mankind. Illustrated. Boards, $1.00.

The Surd of Metaphysics.
An inquiry into the question Are there things-in-themselves?" Cloth, 75c.

T'ai-Shang Kan-Yan P'ien.
Treatise of the Exalted One on response and retribution. Boards, 75c.

Truth and Other Poems.
Truth; Time; Love; De rerum natura; Death. Cloth, $1.00; boards, 50c.

Truth on Trial.
An exposition of the nature of truth, preceded by a critique of pragmatism. Cloth, $1.00; paper, 50c.

The Venus of Milo.
An archeological study of the goddess of womanhood. Illustrated. Cloth, $1.00.

Whence and Whither.
An inquiry into the nature of the soul, its origin and its destiny. Cloth, 75c; paper, 35c.

The World's Parliament of Religions and the Religious Parliament Extension.
A memorial published by the Religious Parliament Extension Committee. Popular edition, 10c.

The Religion of Science.
Cloth, 50c; paper, 30c.

The Open Court Publishing Company
122 South Michigan Avenue :: :: Chicago, Illinois